Piano/Vocal

50 GERSHWIN CLASSICS

Every Time We Say Goodbye (handwritten)

P9-EDJ-246

THEY ALL LAUGHED

Words by
IRA GERSHWIN

Music by
GEORGE GERSHWIN

They all said we nev-er could be hap-py,
They all said we'd nev-er get to-geth-er;

They laughed at us and
Dar-ling, let's take a

how!
bow,

But
For,

Ho, Ho, Ho!
Ho, Ho, Ho!

Who's got the last laugh
Who's got the last laugh,

now?

He, He, He!

Let's at the past laugh,

Ha, Ha, Ha! Who's got the last laugh now?

BY STRAUSS

Words by
IRA GERSHWIN

Music by
GEORGE GERSHWIN

Refrain:

When I want a mel-o-dy lilt-ing through the house,

Then I want a mel-o-dy_____ By Strauss!_____ It

laughs! it sings! The world is in rhyme, Swing-ing to

three quar-ter time._____ Let the "Da-nube" flow a-long And the "Fle-der-

BUT NOT FOR ME

Words by
IRA GERSHWIN

Music by
GEORGE GERSHWIN

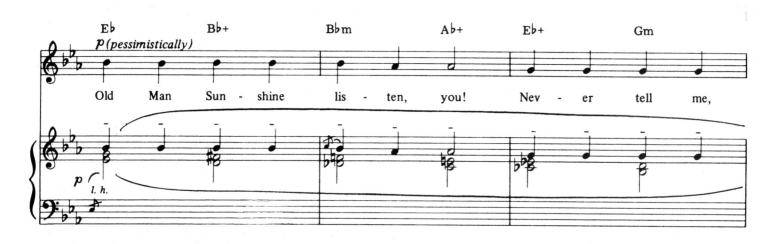

ISN'T IT A PITY

Words by
IRA GERSHWIN

Music by
GEORGE GERSHWIN

NICE WORK IF YOU CAN GET IT

Words by
IRA GERSHWIN

Music by
GEORGE GERSHWIN

The man who on - ly lives for mak - ing mon - ey Lives a life that is - n't nec - es - sa - ri - ly sun - ny. Like - wise the man who works for fame,

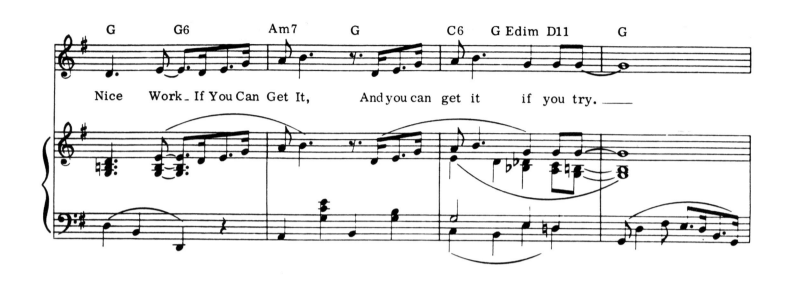

Nice Work If You Can Get It, And you can get it if you try. ___

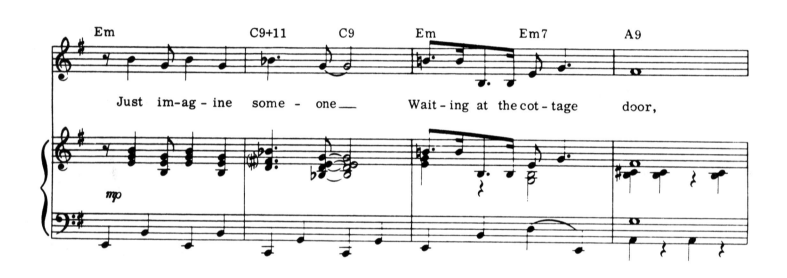

Just im-ag-ine some-one ___ Wait-ing at the cot-tage door,

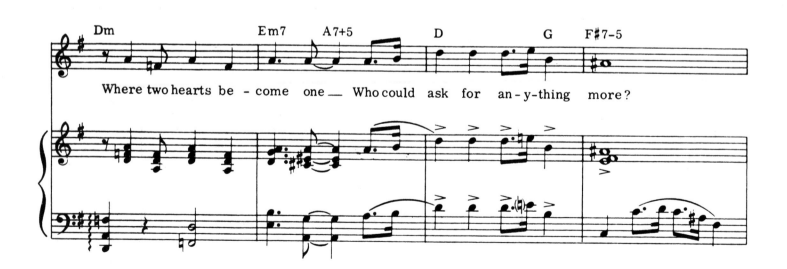

Where two hearts be-come one ___ Who could ask for an-y-thing more?

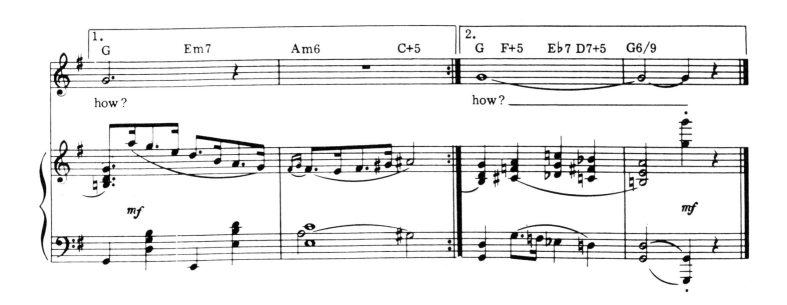

THE MAN I LOVE

Words by
IRA GERSHWIN

Music by
GEORGE GERSHWIN

Andantino semplice

When the mel-low moon be-gins to beam, Ev-'ry night I dream a lit-tle dream,

And of course Prince Charm-ing is the theme, The he for me. Al-

CLAP YO' HANDS

Words by
IRA GERSHWIN

Music by
GEORGE GERSHWIN

HE LOVES AND SHE LOVES

Words by
IRA GERSHWIN

Music by
GEORGE GERSHWIN

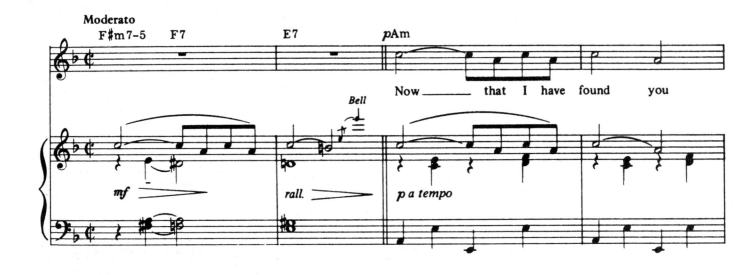

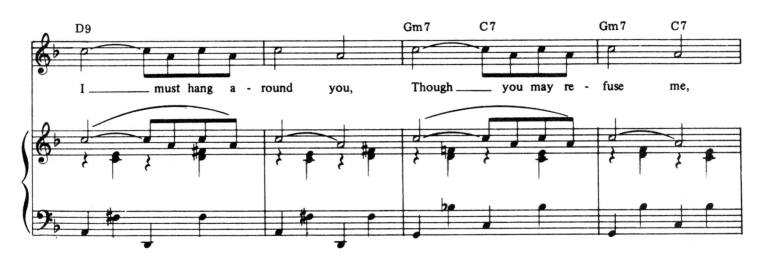

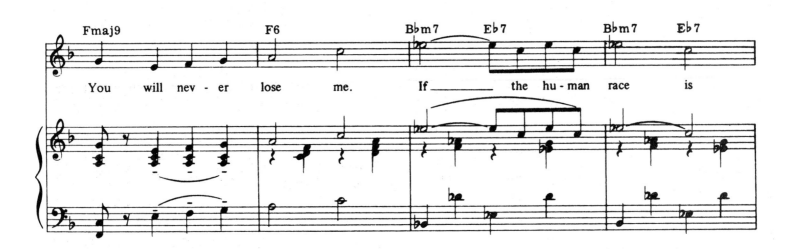

I'VE GOT A CRUSH ON YOU

Words by
IRA GERSHWIN

Music by
GEORGE GERSHWIN

wore down my re-sist-ance: I fell, _____ and it was swell. _____

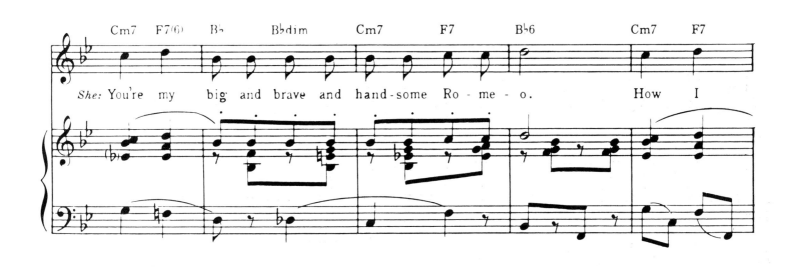

She: You're my big and brave and hand-some Ro-me-o. How I

won you I shall nev-er, nev-er know. *He:* It's not that you're at-trac-tive, But

LOVE IS SWEEPING THE COUNTRY

Words by
IRA GERSHWIN

Music by
GEORGE GERSHWIN

MY ONE AND ONLY (What Am I Gonna Do)

Words by
IRA GERSHWIN

Music by
GEORGE GERSHWIN

PRELUDE I

By
GEORGE GERSHWIN

PRELUDE II

By
GEORGE GERSHWIN

Andante con moto e poco rubato (M.M. ♩ = 88)

* Optional Version: Reverse Hands

PRELUDE III

By
GEORGE GERSHWIN

SWANEE

Words by
IRVING CAESAR

Music by
GEORGE GERSHWIN

WHO CARES?
(SO LONG AS YOU CARE FOR ME)

Words by
IRA GERSHWIN

Music by
GEORGE GERSHWIN

OF THEE I SING

Words by
IRA GERSHWIN

Music by
GEORGE GERSHWIN

Refrain
slowly and with expression

Of thee I sing, ba-by,

Sum-mer, Au-tumn, Win-ter, Spring, ba-by,

You're my sil-ver lin-ing, You're my sky of blue;

There's a love light shin-ing, Just be-cause of you.

HOW LONG HAS THIS BEEN GOING ON?

Words by
IRA GERSHWIN

Music by
GEORGE GERSHWIN

He: As a tot, when I trot-ted in lit-tle vel-vet pant ies,
She: 'Neath the stars at ba-zaars of-ten I've had to ca-ress men,

I was kissed by my sis-ters, my cous-ins and my aunt ies.
Five or ten dol-lars then I'd col-lect from all those yes-men.

Sad to tell, it was Hell, an in-fer-no worse than Dan-te's.
Don't be sad, I must add that they meant no more than chess-men.

MAYBE

Words by
IRA GERSHWIN

Music by
GEORGE GERSHWIN

BIDIN' MY TIME

Words by
IRA GERSHWIN

Music by
GEORGE GERSHWIN

OH, LADY BE GOOD!

Words by
IRA GERSHWIN

Music by
GEORGE GERSHWIN

SWEET AND LOW-DOWN

Words by
IRA GERSHWIN

Music by
GEORGE GERSHWIN

LET'S CALL THE WHOLE THING OFF

Words by
IRA GERSHWIN

Music by
GEORGE GERSHWIN

I go for this and that. Good - ness knows what the

end will be;— Oh, I don't know where I'm at.... It

looks as if we two will nev - er be one,

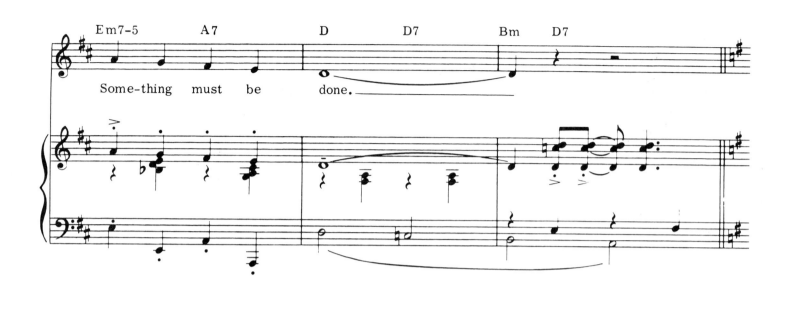

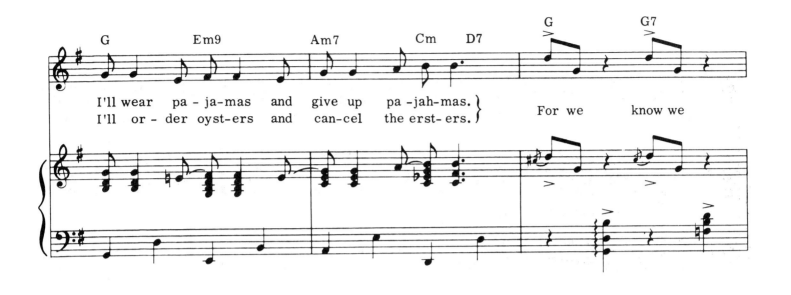

I'll wear pa-ja-mas and give up pa-jah-mas.
I'll or-der oyst-ers and can-cel the erst-ers. } For we know we

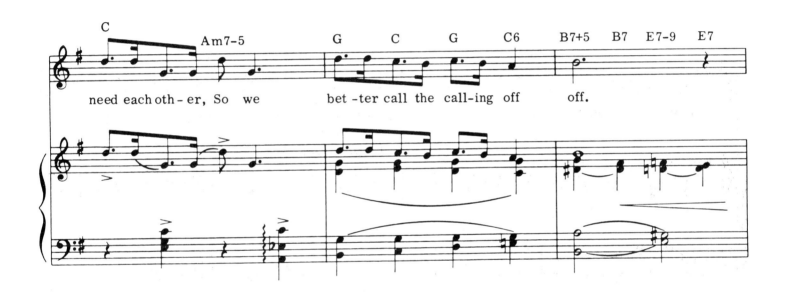

need each oth-er, So we bet-ter call the call-ing off off.

Let's Call The Whole Thing Off! _____ Off! _____

LIZA (All The Clouds'll Roll Away)

Words by
GUS KAHN and IRA GERSHWIN

Music by
GEORGE GERSHWIN

MY COUSIN IN MILWAUKEE

Words by
IRA GERSHWIN

Music by
GEORGE GERSHWIN

sang in a low-down way.   She was a pos-i-tive sen-

sa - tion;   The songs that she sang would nev - er

miss.   My cous - in was my in - spir-

a - tion,   That's how I got like this!

SLAP THAT BASS

Words by
IRA GERSHWIN

Music by
GEORGE GERSHWIN

AN AMERICAN IN PARIS

By
GEORGE GERSHWIN

...one of those warm-hearted, sweeping melodies of which Gershwin held the secret

Blues tempo
Andante ma con ritmo deciso

DO, DO, DO

Words by
IRA GERSHWIN

Music by
GEORGE GERSHWIN

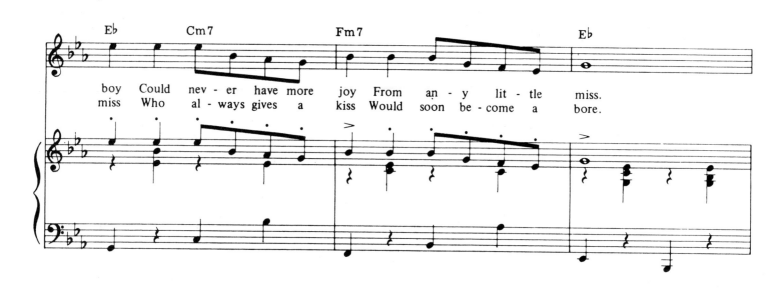

LORELEI

Words by
IRA GERSHWIN

Music by
GEORGE GERSHWIN

I'LL BUILD A STAIRWAY TO PARADISE

Words by
B.G. DeSYLVA and IRA GERSHWIN

Music by
GEORGE GERSHWIN

HIGH HAT

Words by
IRA GERSHWIN

Music by
GEORGE GERSHWIN

Allegro moderato

He: When a fel-low feels he's got to win a girl-ie's hand-ie,

he will send her loads of flow-ers, books and tons of can - dy. *Chorus:* The

o - ver-head is big; oh, how they make us dig!

Put on your gay-est cra-vat,_____

but keep your feet on the ground._____

Oh boy! How they'll come a-round!___ Just treat___ them high

hat!_____ High hat!_____

A FOGGY DAY

Words by
IRA GERSHWIN

Music by
GEORGE GERSHWIN

I was a strang-er in the cit-y.___ Out of town were the peo-ple I knew.

I had that feel-ing of self - pi-ty,___ What to do? What to do? What to do? The

SOMEONE TO WATCH OVER ME

Words by
IRA GERSHWIN

Music by
GEORGE GERSHWIN

DELISHIOUS

Words by
IRA GERSHWIN

Music by
GEORGE GERSHWIN

FUNNY FACE

Words by
IRA GERSHWIN

Music by
GEORGE GERSHWIN

FOR YOU, FOR ME, FOREVERMORE

Words by
IRA GERSHWIN

Music by
GEORGE GERSHWIN

152

THEY CAN'T TAKE THAT AWAY FROM ME

Words by
IRA GERSHWIN

Music by
GEORGE GERSHWIN

'S WONDERFUL

Words by
IRA GERSHWIN

Music by
GEORGE GERSHWIN

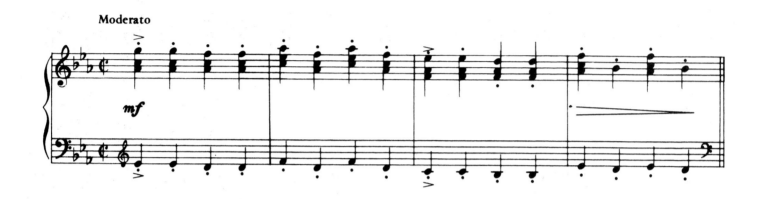

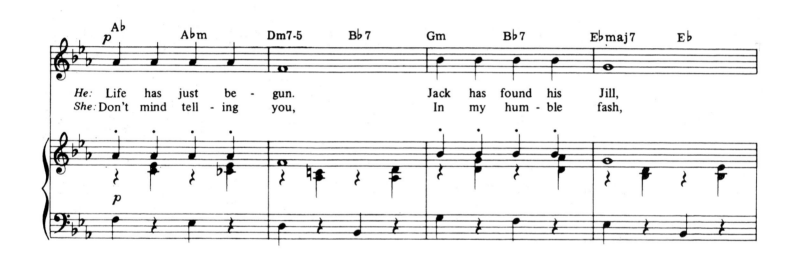

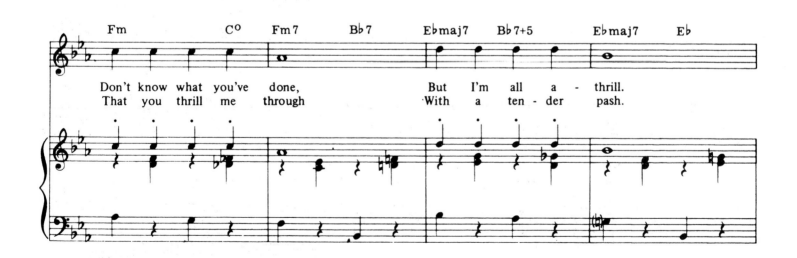

SOON

Words by
IRA GERSHWIN

Music by
GEORGE GERSHWIN

164

DO IT AGAIN!

Words by
B.G. DeSYLVA

Music by
GEORGE GERSHWIN

I GOT RHYTHM

Words by
IRA GERSHWIN

Music by
GEORGE GERSHWIN

REFRAIN (*with abandon*)

LOVE WALKED IN

Words by
IRA GERSHWIN

Music by
GEORGE GERSHWIN

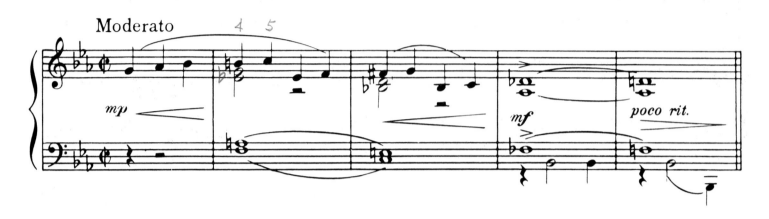

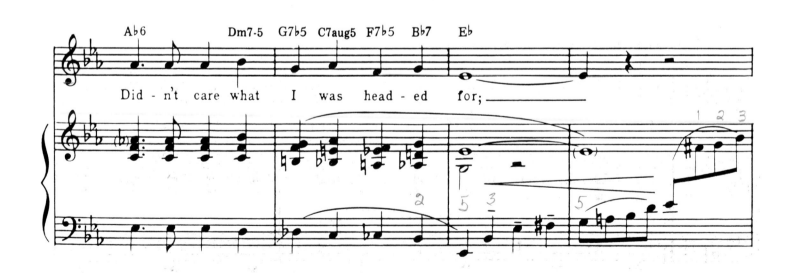

SOMEBODY LOVES ME

Words by
BALLARD MACDONALD and **B.G. DeSYLVA**
French version by EMELIA RENAUD

Music by
GEORGE GERSHWIN

FASCINATING RHYTHM

Words by
IRA GERSHWIN

Music by
GEORGE GERSHWIN

THE HALF OF IT, DEARIE, BLUES

Words by
IRA GERSHWIN

Music by
GEORGE GERSHWIN

(He) Each time you trill a song with Bill, or look at Will, I get a chill— I'm
(She) You dare as-sert that you were hurt each time I'd flirt with Bill or Bert— You

gloom-y. I won't re-call the names of all the men who fall— it's all ap-
brute, you! Well I'm re-paid; I felt be-trayed when an-y maid whom you sur-

-pal-ling to me. Of course I real-ly can-not blame them a bit,—
-veyed would suit you. Com-pared to you, I've been as good as could be—

man-y from whom to choose. _____
an-chor and end your cruise. _____

If you should mar-ry Tom, Dick or Har-ry, Life would be __ the bunk-
You're just a duf-fer Who makes me suf-fer; All the young-er set

I'd be-come a monk. I've got the "You don't know the half of it, dear - ie,"blues!
Says your heart's to let. I've got the "You don't know the half of it, dear - ie,"blues!

RHAPSODY IN BLUE

By
GEORGE GERSHWIN
Paraphrased and Arranged by
HENRY LEVINE

Moderately slow, with expression

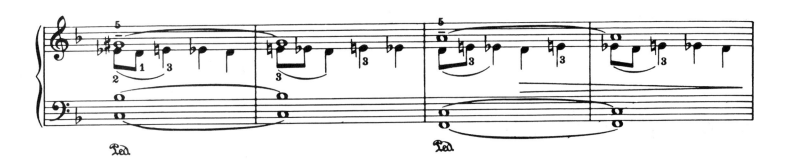

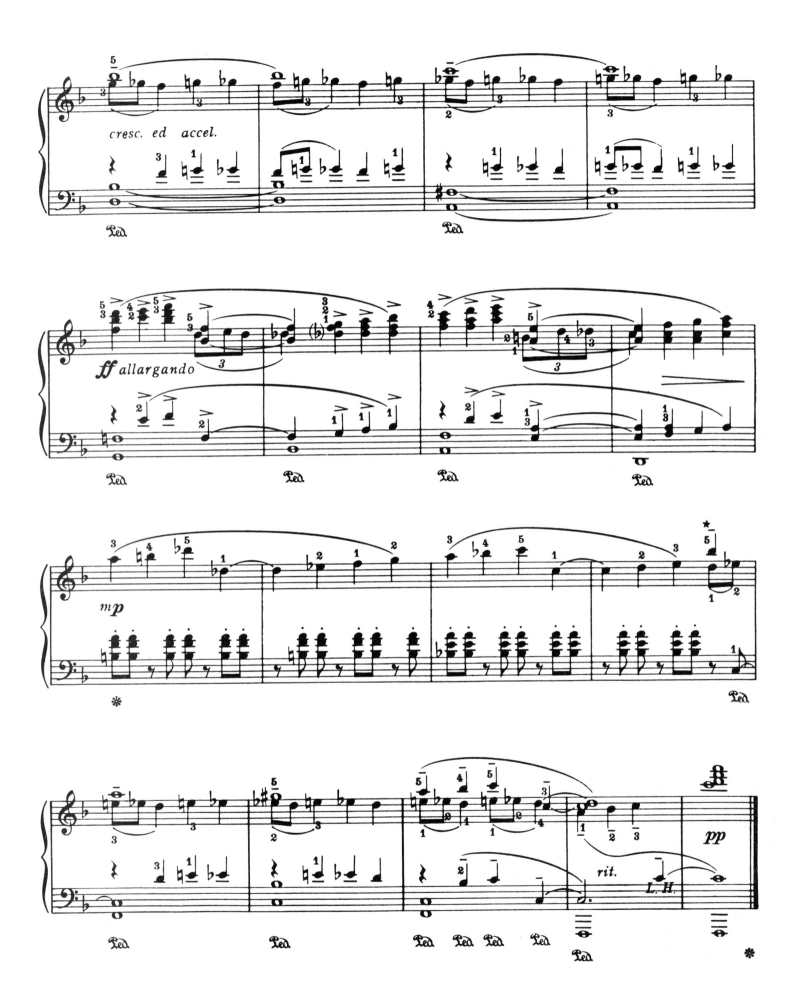

EMBRACEABLE YOU

Words by
IRA GERSHWIN

Music by
GEORGE GERSHWIN

LOVE IS HERE TO STAY

Words by
IRA GERSHWIN

Music by
GEORGE GERSHWIN

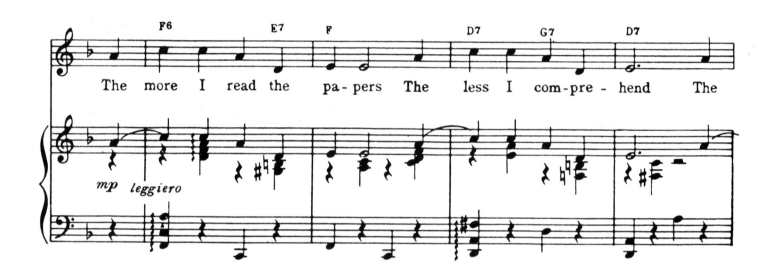

CONCERTO IN F
(SECOND MOVEMENT)

By
GEORGE GERSHWIN

IN THE MANDARIN'S ORCHID GARDEN

Words by
IRA GERSHWIN

Music by
GEORGE GERSHWIN

gai - ly

In the Man-da-rin's or-chid gar-den: ___

The but-ter - cup sighed long - ing-ly,

but love was not for such as she,

And so one day it shriv-eled up and died, still beg-ging par - don,